The Virtual Reality Gallery

Transforming the Art of Exhibition

Table of Contents

Virtual Reality is really a new communication platform. By feeling truly present, you can share unbounded spaces and experiences with the people in your life. Imagine sharing not just moments with your friends online, but entire experiences and adventures.

— Mark Zuckerberg

Chapter 1. Introduction

Welcome to a renaissance in the world of art with our Special Report on "The Virtual Reality Gallery: Transforming the Art of Exhibition." It's not merely about lines or colours anymore; it's an immersive, 360-degree experience that melds the realms of technology and creativity. Prepare to be thrilled as we delve into this new era of artistic interpretation, where you can virtually wander through galleries, view exhibits and sculptures from every angle, and gain insights like never before. Whether you're an art aficionado, a tech-savvy enthusiast, or merely a curious mind, this report will serve as your vibrant, eye-opening ticket to a world where art is not just viewed, but truly experienced. So buckle up! This isn't just about the virtual transformation of art exhibitions; it's a fascinating journey packed with enthusiasm, insights, and revelations that surely will urge you to secure your own special report today!

Chapter 2. The Dawn of Virtual Reality in Arts

As the seamless brush strokes of technology began painting across the canvas of the global art landscape, a new era in arts, that of virtual reality, was born. This convergence of creativity and technology represents the first step into an exciting reality, where exhibitions are not confined by four walls, nor limited by geography, thereby transforming the essence of artistic perception forever.

2.1. The Conception of Virtual Reality

Tracing back the timeline to the conception of Virtual Reality (VR), the fundamental idea of creating a simulated, immersive environment that one can explore and interact with predates the technology that made it possible today by nearly a century. The concept first found life in the 1935 science fiction short story "Pygmalion's Spectacles" by Stanley G. Weinbaum, where a protagonist experiences a holographic, virtual world through a pair of goggles. Today, these 'goggles' are the VR headsets, that transport us into a realm of technologically sculpted beauty.

However, it wasn't until the late 20th century that Virtual Reality started taking a tangible form. The genesis could be attributed to the creation of the 'Sensorama machine' in the 1960s and then to the first head-mounted display system, albeit far from what we have today, in the late 80s. Finally, the 21st century brought with it the requisite technological advancements that have culminated in the VR as we know it today. But still, the union of technology and the arts was yet to be born.

2.2. The Marriage of VR and Arts

The link between technology and artistic presentation is as old as the motion picture itself. The moment, when the first film ushered a new level of creativity, was equally revolutionary as the current advent of VR in arts. The incorporation of VR into art exhibition design was perhaps an inevitable progression, fuelled by the rapidly escalating VR technology developments, and the perennial artistic desire to break barriers and transcend the limitations of conventional presentation modes.

The initial trial phases involved the experimentation with VR's capability to replicate real-world art galleries virtually, such as the Uffizi in Italy, enabling art tourists to explore these spaces from their living rooms. This was perhaps the first open door to the infinite possibilities that VR held for the art world.

2.3. The Transformative Power of VR in Exhibitions

The true potency of virtual reality in arts lies in its capacity to lure the beholder into its immersive world. Rather than being an observer, a participatory role is adopted where one feels part of the artwork rather than merely a spectator. This seismic shift, from an observational standpoint to a participatory one, leads to a much deeper connection and understanding between the viewer and the art piece or exhibition.

VR in arts presents an entirely new dimension, where art is not just visually perceived but genuinely experienced. It provides a unique platform for artists and curators to explore less conventional narratives and layouts, defy the laws of physics, and build settings that would be impossible in physical reality. What started as a ripple in the vast ocean of arts has today transformed into waves of revolution promising a colourful panorama of limitless imaginational explorations.

2.4. The Architectural Impact

With VR's inception, the concept of infrastructural confines was shattered. Why restrict artwork within white-walled galleries when you can curate an exhibition amongst celestial bodies? The potential for curators and artists to not only display art in unconventional settings but also to create art specifically for such settings opened up limitless vistas for the viewer and for art itself.

Not just that, the technological marvel of VR also allows artists to engage with the concept of architecture and space in a refreshingly different manner. They can challenge, manipulate or even completely disregard conventional architectural rules to create art that creates a viewer experience that physical galleries might not be able to.

In conclusion, the dawn of VR in arts has brought with it a whirlwind of change and infinite possibilities, transforming the viewing experience into an increasingly participative one, breaking the barriers of geography and physical space, and continuously redefining the very essence of exhibition design. Hold on to your VR headsets as this whirlwind is only set to intensify, promising futures hitherto unimagined.

Remember, whether you are an art enthusiast, novice, or seasoned professional, the exciting world of VR in arts is perched on a precipice of limitless possibilities and boundless creativity. It's a transformative revolution, and it has only just begun.

Chapter 3. Evolution of Exhibition : From Physical to Digital

The journey of art from canvas to screen, from the palpable to the digital sphere, is an astonishing one, deeply rooted in the essence of human creativity and our penchant for innovation. This evolution offers an intriguing overview of not just the shifting landscapes of art, but also of cultural perception, artist-audience interaction, and mounting technological advancements.

3.1. Tracing the Ancients: The Genesis of Exhibitions

Traditionally, the display and exhibition of art forms were confined to sanctum sanctorum, royal courts, and eventually, the modern museums. A sense of exclusivity was at play; from cave paintings of prehistoric times to the majestic sculptures of Mesopotamia and paintings adorning the walls of Egyptian tombs, art was mostly shrouded in ritualistic and regal mysteries.

The earliest semblance of 'public galleries' took shape during the Renaissance period. Artists ventured beyond chapels and royal households, and art gradually pervaded the social fabric. Exemplars such as the Uffizi Gallery, established in the 16th century Florence, offered a gallery-esque experience. However, it wasn't until the advent of Kunstmuseum in Switzerland in 1661 that the true public "art museum" was born. This marked the commencement of a more democratic environment for art—and its reception.

3.2. The Rise and Transformation of the Modern Museum

The emergence of the Modern Museum in the 18th and 19th centuries saw art become a topic of public discourse. Galleries fostered social and cultural discussions, allowing various interpretations to thrive. Places like the British Museum London, the Louvre Paris, or the State Hermitage Museum in Saint Petersburg, became cultural landmarks in their cities, shaping the identity of their locations.

But these exhibitions were still not devoid of limitations. Space constraints, geographic barriers, and financial issues posed challenges to both curators and enthusiasts. Art remained largely inaccessible to a significant portion of the globe, turning the enjoyment of art into a privilege rather than a universally available pleasure.

3.3. The Advent of Technology: A New Dimension Emerges

Advancements in technology provided a solution to these limitations. As the 20th century unfurled, radio broadcasts and television screens brought performances and concerts into people's homes. However, fine arts—paintings, sculptures, installations—remained tethered to their physical locations until the advent of the internet.

Suddenly, geographical barriers seemed less imposing. Online galleries began to surface, offering a new avenue for artists to showcase their work and viewers to explore global art—without having to catch the next flight. 'The Louvre Online', conceived in the late 1990s, propelled this concept into mainstream discourse, paving the way for an era where the physical and the digital coalesce.

3.4. Fine-tuning the Digital Experience: The Next Phase of Evolution

Enter the 21st century, and we find ourselves at the precipice of yet another revolutionary transition. While online galleries offered the visual aspect of art, they couldn't offer the intimate, immersive experience of strolling through an actual gallery space. Turning this shortcoming into an opportunity, Virtual Reality (VR) stepped into the frame to usher in a new facet of digital evolution.

Virtual Reality Galleries provide an immersive, 360-degree view of art, transcending the 2D constraints of conventional online platforms. By strapping on a VR headset, art enthusiasts are teleported to an interactive dimension where they can appreciate art from every angle, almost as if they were physically present at the site.

3.5. Epilogue - Media Transcendence: The Digital Wave Recasts Artistic Experience

With this parallel universe, the physical-turned-digital art exhibition has evolved to an immersive, accessible platform that transcends geographical, financial, and temporal barriers—a testament to the human spirit's capacity to adapt and innovate. Creatives are exploring these virtual spaces, positing their ideas and expressions in equal parts reality and virtuality. Art lovers, irrespective of their location, can dive into these digital marvels, experiencing and interacting with art like never before.

Indeed, the evolution of exhibitions from physical to digital is our modern Odyssey—an immense voyage into uncharted territories, a testament to the human spirit's inventiveness. Today, we stand at a fascinating crossroads where creativity meets technology, an enthralling intersection that promises resplendent vistas ahead.

In our next chapter, we will pull away the veil of mystery from this fascinating tech tool and discuss the intricacies of technology powering Virtual Reality art galleries. So, sit back, brace yourself and prepare to be amazed as we embark on a deeper exploration of this art-technology interface.

Chapter 4. Behind the Virtual Curtain: The Technology Powering VR Galleries

Virtual Reality (VR) continues to make waves in numerous industries, and the art gallery sphere is no exception. The core of this digital revolution lies in the advanced, intricate technologies empowering these immersive experiences. Let's take a gaze beyond the veil and explore the world of VR technology enhancing the way we perceive art.

4.1. The Mechanics of Virtual Reality

VR technology employs several complex mechanisms designed to create an immersive environment that feels authentic and tangible. At its heart, the technology demands high computing power to render lifelike 3D graphics, creating an illusion of depth and scale that simulates our perception of the real world.

State-of-the-art VR headsets house two small LCD monitors, each projected at one eye, producing stereoscopic images. Breaking down this concept further, stereoscopy works on binocular vision - an aspect of human sight in which both eyes perceive an object from slightly different angles. This dual perspective translates to the brain as a singular image with depth and dimension – an effect VR strives to replicate electronically.

The headsets sync these images, rendered multiple times per second, with the users' movements employing sensors and cameras. This interactive functionality ensures a real-time, responsive VR environment. Likewise, specialized audio units provide 3D sound to add yet another credible layer to the user's immersion.

4.2. Virtual Galleries: Transforming Physical To Digital

Digital reproduction is fundamental in the creation of VR galleries. Artists and curators collaborate with technologists to digitize art into 3D models using photogrammetry, a technique capturing high-resolution images from numerous angles to generate a comprehensive digital replica. High-quality 3D scanners also play a significant role by capturing the minute details of a piece.

Subsequently, these digital files are refined using 3D modeling software and then incorporated into a virtual environment designed using an assortment of VR development tools. Such environments can mimic the look and feel of a physical gallery – replicating not just the artworks, but also the lighting, layout, background noise, and sometimes even the weather outside viewed through the gallery's windows, virtually crafting a holistic artistic encounter.

4.3. Perception of Depth, Distance, and Proximity

Precision is an essential element in VR. It revolves around accurately calibrating light, shadows, textures, and spatial sound – particularly when interpreting depth and distance. Specialized software tools extrapolate these aspects, including an object's position, distance, and size, and translate them into multi-sensory data that the human brain can perceive.

Furthermore, the VR sense of proximity assures that as users approach or retreat from an art piece, the corresponding variations in visual and auditory feedback align with reality. This kind of attention to detail ensures a stimulating, authentic experience for the virtual visitor.

4.4. VR Devices and Accessibility

While VR technology does require specific equipment, its embrace of diversity and accessibility remains impressive. Currently, VR experiences cater to standard VR devices such as the Oculus Rift, HTC Vive, and PlayStation VR. Meanwhile, smartphone-powered apparatuses like the Samsung Gear VR or Google Cardboard make the technology accessible at a lower price.

VR also embraces a multi-platform approach, with many VR galleries offering compatibility across various systems. These inclusive efforts are crucial in democratizing technology and increasing accessibility for larger audiences, bridging the gap between the tech-savvy and those poised on the peripheries of the digital divide.

4.5. The Role of Haptic Feedback

Haptic technology – the provision of tangible feedback through sensation – introduces another facet to VR immersion by invoking the sense of touch. Haptic feedback devices can mimic the sensation of texture, weight, and resistance, enhancing the tactile dimensions of the virtual gallery visit. However, in respect for the inviolable principle of the art world, 'do not touch the artworks', these sensations are mostly reserved for the virtual gallery environment outside the artworks themselves.

Behind the virtual curtain lies a world shimmering with cutting-edge technologies sculpting immersive virtual galleries. Far from being a sudden leap, this digital evolution has been gradually strengthened over the years. Before our very eyes, VR emerges from its technological chrysalis, unfolding as an entity identifying as much with the cerulean pixels of technology as with the visceral hues of human creativity, transforming how we perceive, participate and revel in the world of art, one virtual gallery at a time.

Chapter 5. The Artistic Experience: Immersion and Interactivity in Virtual Reality

The realm of art is a universe unto itself; an infinite expanse that overflows with the profound echoes of creative thought and illuminating expression. Human creativity has now grappled with the powerful forces of technology, and this matrimony has birthed a new era of art exhibition – the Virtual Reality Art Gallery. It is here that the tangible and intangible blur into one another, creating a whole new artistic experience defined largely by two key facets – immersion and interactivity.

5.1. The Landscape of Immersion

Immersion in the context of Virtual Reality (VR) can be likened to an individual's deep dive into the blue ocean, engrossed in its depth and tranquillity. However, instead of a natural aquatic atmosphere, immersion in VR transports one into a realm constructed digitally. This digital realm exhibits an infinite array of artistic forms, colours, and textures, and even breathes life into still art.

Through the lens of a VR headset, viewers are no longer confined to the physical limitations of a conventional art gallery. Art pieces are liberated from the immovable hooks on gallery walls. A photograph locked into a frame, for example, transforms into an astonishingly tangible landscape where you can explore every detail up close. From the fluttering of leaves hanging on the trees, to the shimmering sunlight scattering off a riverbed, the viewer becomes an integral part of the exhibit.

5.2. Breathing Life Into Interactivity

Complementing the all-consuming nature of immersion is the second key tenet of VR– interactivity. It is one factor to observe and admire an exquisite piece of art, but an entirely fresh and intoxicating experience to actively engage with it. The boundaries dissipate between the viewer and the viewed, paving the way for a more transcendental and intimate relationship with art.

Interactivity spans various dimensions in VR art galleries ranging from the manipulation of objects, surroundings, to audio-visual cues. Imagine standing in front of Michelangelo's 'David' and having the power to deconstruct the sculpture with a wave of your hand, examining each piece individually and understanding the mastery involved in the original composition. Or, imagine strolling through one of Monet's water lily paintings, immersing yourself in its blooming flowers, brushing against the delicate petals, listening to the gentle wash of the surrounding pond and the harmonic hum of nature; all while still being at the comfort of your living room.

5.3. Immersion and Interactivity in the Light of Virtual Technology

Virtual Reality technology serves as the fulcrum, balancing the immersive and interactive elements and interweaving them into a seamless fabric of artistic experience. Immersion speaks to our senses, tricking the mind into believing the artificial as real, while interactivity redefines the idea of viewer participation, evolving it from passive admiration to active engagement.

Technological advancements in VR ranging from headsets to gloves equipped with haptic feedback, spatial audio advancements, and even progress made in the field of olfactory VR collectively contribute to this enveloping world of immersive interactivity.

5.4. In Conclusion

Art has ceaselessly strived for the utmost engagement with audiences over the centuries. However, it is interesting to ponder here that art's struggle to engage finds liberation in the realms of Virtual Reality. Immersion and interactivity blend together to create a transformative art viewing experience; an experience that redefines the age-old interaction between the artist, the artwork, and the viewer. This shift, welcomed by the 21st century's embrace of Virtual Reality art galleries, suffuses fresh life into the static world of traditional art expressions, opening doors to a future where art will not just be viewed, but truly felt, touched, heard, and lived.

Chapter 6. Practical Use Cases: Virtual Galleries Around the World

In the grand tapestry of art evolution, one of the most captivating developments has been the migration of traditional galleries into the digital sphere, particularly in the realm of Virtual Reality (VR). This chapter will explore practical use cases of VR galleries across the world, examining how they've harnessed the power of technology to re-invent the art-viewing experience.

6.1. A Global Tour through VR Galleries

Navigating the geographical barriers of traditional art exhibitions, VR offers an unprecedented opportunity to voyage across national and cultural borders without stepping a foot outside. In the subsequent paragraphs, we will peer into some of the VR galleries worldwide that have transmogrified the art experience.

Arguably one of the pioneers, the British Museum, featuring its well-crafted VR gallery, The Bronze Age roundhouse, transports users back in time. In the virtual space, patrons can grab objects, inspecting them meticulously, and gain insights from accompanying scholarly commentary, an experience difficult to replicate in a physical setting.

This transformative experience has also echoed within the halls of the prestigious Uffizi Gallery in Florence. In partnership with Indiana University, the gallery took digitization a step further with their VR venture into the famous Niobe room, enabling remote patrons to fully immerse themselves amidst Renaissance masterpieces.

Over in the States, The Kremer Museum, a private collection of 17th-century Dutch and Flemish art, has been entirely rebirthed in VR. Built using photogrammetry and CGI, the Museum's virtual avatar now provides an unparalleled three-dimensional look at the artworks, bringing a richer vividness and depth to the collection.

6.2. Enriching Education in Arts

Use of VR in the art world isn't restricted to global tours; it carries transformative implications for art education as well.

Institutions such as the Art Institute of Chicago and the Los Angeles County Museum of Art have introduced VR in their pedagogical methodology, designing virtual apprenticeships where learners can study artworks up close, foster a deeper understanding of artistic technique, and intimately explore historical contexts that surround each piece.

Additionally, universities globally are integrating VR into coursework. An example is the course at Pennsylvania State University which employs VR to teach spatial literacy and three-dimensional thinking. Students virtually explore artworks, producing 3D models that help them understand spatial relationships, an essential skill in appreciating and creating art.

6.3. A Tool for Inclusivity

While we've seen how VR can be used to transcend geographical barriers, it has also emerged as a powerful ally for art accessibility.

Persons with disabilities or those who endure physical impairments that limit fine motor skills can now engage with art in different ways through VR. Virtual tours of galleries, coupled with features like audio commentary, enable people with visual issues to absorb and appreciate art, regardless of their geographical location. Equally, those with auditory challenges can utilize subtitled curator guides, ensuring an inclusive art experience.

6.4. Immersive Storytelling

VR galleries are not only about replicating physical art spaces; they also provide an expansive platform for storytelling through immersive content.

Forefronting this approach, The Metropolitan Museum of Art launched a virtual exhibition called "Cantor Roof Garden Commission," embracing VR's potential to illustrate narrative. Visitors don VR headsets to experience and interact with artist Alicja Kwade's celestial-themed installations, catapulted into a virtual cosmic voyage that blends the boundaries of art and science.

Unquestionably, Virtual Reality has validated itself as more than a mere technology. It has become a robust means of making art more accessible, educational, and inclusive. As we step towards an ever-evolving future, it promises to continually reshape our collective artistic experience, ushering in an exhilarating new era of creativity. Today, we're at the cusp of this digital revolution where the entire world can be our gallery, and every day becomes an artistic adventure.

Chapter 7. Art Accessibility and Learning through Virtual Reality

Our journey across the realms of art and technology introduces us to the potent and transformative subject of art accessibility and learning through virtual reality (VR). This chapter encompasses both the theoretical and practical aspects of assessing and appreciating art via a virtual medium. From defining the concept of accessibility within the sphere of visual arts to exploring how virtual reality helps mitigate barriers and even equips us with an enhanced understanding of art, we shall travel the many pathways this radical technology holds for us.

7.1. Expanding Accessibility through VR Technology

In the traditional sense, accessibility in art has often referred to the ability of an individual to physically reach, perceive, and connect with a piece of art. Accessibility is confined not only by the geographical location of the physical gallery but also by other factors that prevent certain people from experiencing this art fully. These include, but are not limited to, disabilities, lack of socio-economic resources, and an absence of systemic support and understanding of diverse perspectives.

However, VR technology redefines the concept of accessibility, extending it beyond physical access to a degree that has never been possible before. VR permits a shift from physical to comprehensive and inclusive access, allowing the viewer to bypass traditional gallery restrictions and barriers. It paves the way for a universal platform where art can be experienced from any corner of the planet, thus eliminating the geographical constraint that a physical gallery represents. In essence, VR technology is not just about revolutionising the physical experience; it's about creating an open and inclusive space, eradicating traditional barriers of access to the world of art.

7.2. Reinventing Art Education with Virtual Reality

Art education, traditionally, has been a process that required a physical learning environment involving in-person instructions, hands-on experiences, and live interactions. However, with VR technology, art education is changing its conventional form, becoming an immersive and interactive experience that facilitates a more profound understanding of art.

Virtual reality, combined with educational content, creates a dynamic learning experience and highlights new perspectives in art studies. By navigating a virtual gallery, students can observe a piece of art from infinite angles, get closer than typically permitted physically, and even penetrate the art in some cases. This in-depth exploration facilitates a holistic understanding of the artwork, promoting active learning and kindling curiosity in ways previously unimagined.

Further, the inclusion of metadata and interactive content enhances the learning experience. A VR platform can provide instant access to the background information of an artwork, understanding the context and history of the piece, and often the artist's thoughts about their own work. This multi-faceted learning approach via VR can accommodate various learning styles and preferences.

7.3. Case Studies: Virtual Reality-based Art Learning Programs

Examining real-life instances of VR implementing virtual reality for art education provides valuable insights into this phenomenon. We identify two such cases for detailed examination.

In 2018, the British Museum, in partnership with Oculus, launched a VR education program – the Virtual Egyptian Temple. The program completely transformed the traditional school trip into an exhilarating VR experience, bringing ancient culture to life. Students could virtually walk around the temple, closely observe hieroglyphics and ancient artifacts — experiences they couldn't have received in a traditional museum setting.

Another example is of The Kremer Collection launching a VR museum in 2017. Housing masterpieces of Dutch and Flemish artists, this VR museum enhances the art-learning experience by offering private tours, guided by artificial intelligence, illuminating details about the displayed pieces and their history.

These pioneering efforts showcase how VR has made significant strides in art education, foreshadowing its potential.

7.4. Future Implications of VR for Reimagining Accessibility and Art Learning

VR revolutionizes accessibility in art and usurps conventional methods of art education. This offers both opportunities and challenges as we advance into the virtual world. It's essential to address the need for digital literacy, issues of affordability, and training in VR technology to provide an equitable and inclusive experience to all.

The spectrum of art accessibility and learning via VR is vast and promising. It has the potential to educate, engage and inspire participants on a global level, making art more democratic. Embracing these developments and technological possibilities will pave the way for a future where art not only transcends geographical and physical boundaries but also breaks down barriers of exclusivity, making it a shareable, accessible, and universal experience, one in which we all can partake regardless of our individual circumstances.

As we delve deeper into this subfield, we see an unprecedented opportunity for growth. Embracing these virtual developments and technological possibilities will equip us with the tools to educate and illuminate future generations in remarkable new ways. VR presents us with a fresh, immersive, and exciting trail in the world of art and education — one that we are just beginning to traverse.

Chapter 8. Inclusion and Diversity: How VR Level the Playing Field

Today's world is characterized by an increasing call for inclusivity and diversity. This call has profoundly echoed in practically every facet of society, and the art world is no different. Innovation and creativity are essential keys to fostering diversity, and Virtual Reality (VR) conveniently provides a platform for these keys to flourish. Being more than just a facet of advanced technology, VR is a transformative tool that ensures accessibility and diversity in art, levelling the playing field for all.

8.1. The Leverage of Virtual Reality for Inclusion

Traditionally, exhibitions, galleries, and museums have been locations that are unfortunately geographically limiting, thereby affecting inclusivity in the art world. Several individuals don't get to indulge their interest or passion for art simply because they are far removed from the locations where the exhibits are held. VR technology is a game changer, bridging this geographical divide significantly. Now, art can be accessed from anywhere; all that is required is a VR headset and an Internet connection.

VR has essentially eliminated borders, thus removing the geographical limitations and allowing people to have access to art galleries, exhibits and installations around the world. This potent tool has effectively broadened the horizons of the art world, making it more accessible and leveling the playing field for enthusiasts and artists alike.

8.2. Diversity: A Rich Tapestry of Artistic Talent

Virtual Reality is not only inclusive; it also serves as a vehicle to promote diversity in art. Art reflects society, and like society, it is rich and diverse. The challenge, though, is providing visibility for all these diverse voices. Curation practices at traditional galleries have often been accused of bias, either consciously or unconsciously. This has sometimes led to a narrow representation of artistic expressions.

VR is transforming this landscape by providing an unbiased platform where more voices can be heard. This technology helps ensure that artists from marginalized groups get their fair share of visibility without the constraints that are often found in traditional art spheres. Artists of different genders, races, and socio-economic backgrounds can now produce, exhibit, and sell their work in virtual galleries, thus breaking boundaries and shifting the narrative towards a more diverse representation.

8.3. Amplifying Interaction: The Key to Inclusion

Aside from providing visibility, VR has presented the world with another essential facet of inclusion: interaction. Traditional physical galleries are limiting because visitors cannot physically touch or experience most art forms due to their delicate nature. With VR, this changes dramatically.

Virtual Reality allows users to engage with the art pieces in a more interactive and immersive manner. They can view a piece of artwork from different angles, zoom into intricate details, and sometimes even experience the art creation process from the artist's perspective - all without risking any harm to the artwork. This heightened level of interaction lends more inclusivity to the art world and transforms the experience from just a viewing exercise to a deeply personal one.

8.4. Conclusion: The Virtual Reality Revolution

In conclusion, the symbiosis between art and technology through VR is undoubtedly impacting the world of art, exhibition, and education. The once exclusive and elitist space of art is being transformed into a more inclusive and diverse domain through the VR revolution. Artists from different backgrounds are presented with an opportunity to find a space where their work can exist and be celebrated, defying the typical constraints of the traditional art exhibition landscape.

Moreover, the interactive and immersive nature offered by VR creates a fascinating, unique experience that invites greater viewer participation. By harnessing the power of VR, every individual, irrespective of their geographical, socio-economic or physical barriers, has an opportunity to engage with and appreciate the rich diversity of artwork that our world has to offer.

In a nutshell, Virtual Reality demonstrates the potential to transform the world of art and culture with its unifying power, bridging the gap between access and opportunity. It's ushering a new era for artists and audiences, fostering an enriched art experience that transcends physical boundaries and promotes inclusivity and diversity.

Chapter 9. The Impact on Artists: Opportunities and Challenges in Creating VR Art

In the floodlight of the modern artistic era, artists find themselves at the intersection where technology is no longer considered an interloper but a companion, an ally. We now enter a new realm of discussion, where the brush and the pixel coalesce. Welcome to the exploration of how the incorporation of Virtual Reality (VR) has moulded the creative landscape for artists. From the wide canvases of opportunities it presents to the challenging precipices it casts, VR has unfolded a new era for creators globally.

9.1. Unleashing Boundless Creativity

One of the most salient opportunities presented by VR artistry is the scope for boundless creativity. The traditional constraints of physical media - the canvas, the paint, the brushes - are no longer a limiting factor. The VR environment provides artists with near-endless space to convey their vision. They can defy the laws of physics, blending and bending both time and space to create works that could never be replicated in a tangible environment. This elevation from the constraint of physical mediums encourages experimentation and drives innovation.

Artists can now also incorporate elements of motion and change into their artworks, allowing for the expression of ideas through dynamic, rather than static, compositions. The beauty of a blossoming flower, the gentle flap of a butterfly's wings, or the evocative unspooling of smoke can now be immortalized, not just in a single moment, but as a continuous narrative, in a mesmerizing choreography of experiences.

9.2. Enhancing the Artistic Narrative

Developments in VR technology have also transcended the conventional one-dimensional viewing experience. Unlike traditional art forms, VR artistry can be incredibly immersive and interactive. Artists now have the powerful tool to guide viewers along a specific narrative or journey within their creation, thereby offering a more profound emotional engagement.

9.3. The Path of Interactivity

Viewers can interact with the art pieces in ways previously unthinkable. From repositioning elements, changing perspectives, shading light from different angles, to experiencing different textures, the VR platform expands the realms of viewer interaction. This newfound creative freedom opens the doors for artists to engage with their audience in a novel and more intimate way.

9.4. Opportunities for Artistic Collaboration

VR technology does not just empower individual creativity but also catalyses collective innovation. The digital nature of VR creations allows several artists to collaborate on the same piece, even if they are physically spread across different time zones. The power to bring together diverse perspectives transcends geographical limitations and harbors an unprecedented degree of cooperative creativity.

9.5. Challenges in the VR Landscape

Despite the wealth of opportunities, like any nascent frontier, the VR artistic realm is not devoid of challenges. A significant hurdle artists often face is the steep learning curve associated with mastering the technology. It requires a unique blend of skills, combining the traditional artistry prowess with a grasp of new software and tools.

The cost of VR technology is not inconsequential either. The software, hardware, and accessories required to either create or view VR art can be a considerable investment. While the prices have been gradually declining over the years, they still pose a significant barrier for many budding or economically disadvantaged artists.

9.6. The Perils of Intangibility

Another issue arises from the intangible nature of VR art – how does one preserve the integrity of the artwork? If an artwork only exists in a virtual space, its replication or modification poses a significant challenge. Artists are forced to consider the implications of intellectual property rights in this new and relatively unregulated space.

9.7. Navigating Audience Reception

Even for those artists who can navigate the technological and financial hurdles, understanding and predicting audience reception to VR art presents a further predicament. VR art demands viewers to actively engage and immerse themselves in the artwork, which can be daunting for those unaccustomed or resistant to this new, interactive mode of artistic consumption.

9.8. The Future for VR Art Creation

As we stride further into the digital age, it becomes evident that the lines that once segregated technology and artistry are blurring. VR, with all its opportunities and challenges, is reshaping the landscape for artists around the world. It is fostering a new brilliance in the art world, a renaissance of sorts, one illuminated by the glow of pixels and the rhythm of code.

Despite the existing hurdles, the possibility for boundless creativity, immersive narratives, increased viewer engagement, and global collaborations offers a compelling future for VR in art. It truly is an exciting epoch for artists to harness this technology and pioneer a realm of possibilities hitherto unheard of in the traditional art setting.

As more artists explore and embrace VR as their canvas, the potential for a vibrant, tech-infused, artistic landscape only amplifies. The mysteries of the virtual realm have merely started to unspool, heralding an incredible journey into the depths of creativity, ultimately forging a new reality in art – a virtual reality. The exciting potential nestled within this virtual sphere is immeasurable and profound, sparking a paradigm shift in how art might operate in the digital age.

Chapter 10. Future Trends: The Coming Era of Augmented Reality Galleries

As we venture further into our exploration of the futuristic world of visual arts, we unearth an astounding facet that reframes our understanding of immersive experiences - Augmented Reality (AR). Unlike the completely simulated environments of VR, AR overlays digital information onto the real world, thereby offering a blend of physical and virtual realms. In the area of art exhibitions, this technology holds great promise, set to redefine not just the way we exhibit and view art, but also how we acquire, learn about, and engage with it.

10.1. The Concept and Scope of AR in Art Galleries

Augmented Reality, often seen as a sister technology to VR, adds a layer of digital enrichment to our physical world. Within the context of an art gallery, this could involve overlaying additional details onto a sculpture or painting, providing viewers with real-time analysis and information, or embedding interactive elements.

The scope of AR in art galleries is profoundly extensive. It offers the potential to transform static artwork into dynamic interfaces that can interact with the viewer, democratize access to art, and unlock new revenue streams for artists and galleries. With these vistas of possibilities opening up, we find AR pushing the traditional boundaries of art exhibition and consumption.

10.2. Art Comes to Life with AR

One of the most exciting aspects of AR in art galleries is the potential to bring artworks to life. Imagine standing in front of a painting and having animated figures from the artwork stepping out onto your smartphone screen, providing a story or delivering monologues linked to the artwork.

This technology can also transform sculptures into dynamic, interactive entities. Viewers could manipulate the virtual overlay using motion-sensing technology, altering the sculpture's perceived shape, colour, or texture. By superseding the inherent 'distance' associated with traditional art viewing, AR fundamentally alters the dynamics of art appreciation, making it an active, participatory experience.

10.3. AR for Art Education and Accessibility

Apart from transforming the way people view and interact with art, AR also holds significant potential for art education and accessibility. For instance, it can display artist biographies, historical backgrounds of artworks, or thematic analyses directly onto the viewer's screen, enhancing their understanding.

Furthermore, AR can aid in making art more accessible for people with disabilities. By overlaying captions or sign language interpretations onto artworks, it can enhance the experience for the hearing-impaired. For the visually impaired, an AR app could provide descriptive audio narrations or enable the exploration of textured, virtual replicas of artworks.

10.4. AR for Marketing and Sales in the Art World

AR technology extends far beyond creating engaging and immersive experiences. It also comes as a potent tool for marketing and sales in the art world. Galleries can create AR experiences to virtually showcase their collections to prospective buyers, offering an enriched browsing experience that goes beyond static images or videos. In an era where digital purchase of art has seen a rise, AR can enhance customer confidence by offering virtual 'view-in-room' capabilities.

10.5. Challenges on the Path to AR Adoption

Though the possibilities seem unlimited, the path to widespread adoption of AR in art galleries isn't free from challenges. Technical limitations, such as maintaining accurate alignment of digital overlays, ensuring high-quality renderings, and producing effective user interfaces, must be overcome. Moreover, the upfront cost of investing in AR development may be prohibitive for smaller galleries or individual artists.

The idea of tampering with an aesthetic experience through digital overlays raises myriad questions about the sanctity and authenticity of the art experience. Acceptance from the art community is vital for this technology to gain traction.

10.6. Looking Ahead: The Future of AR Galleries

As we look forward to the future of art exhibition, we can envision a world where physical galleries become augmentation-friendly spaces, filled with beacon technology, QR codes, and other interactive elements. Virtual galleries could offer AR experiences that interact with the user's surroundings, making art an integrated part of our everyday lives.

There is no denying that Augmented Reality presents a paradigm shift in the way we perceive the boundaries of art, challenge the concepts of space and interaction, and redefine the art exhibition. With the relentless advancements in technology, the day isn't far when the thin line between our physical reality and augmented experiences blurs completely, and we find ourselves submerged in the vibrant continuum of augmented art.

In conclusion, the advent of AR in the art world echoes the constant evolution of technology and creativity. As we stand at the intersection of art and technology, the prospect of exploring Augmented Reality Galleries leaves us in awe and anticipation, compelling us to embrace the future with open arms and open minds, forever changing our approach to art and its interpretation.

Chapter 11. Afterword: The Intersection of Art and Technology in the Age of Virtual Reality

As we draw the curtain on this comprehensive account of the intersection of virtual reality (VR) and the art world, it's appropriate to look back at the leaps and bounds we've made. We've traversed the journey from virtual reality's nascent stages in the art, through its current interpretation, and peeked at the robust future that awaits us. This transformation certainly begs the question: How has this intersection reshaped our understanding of art, and what would the ramifications be in the progressive age of VR?

11.1. The Recalibration of Artistic Perception

VR has indisputably bid goodbye to dated constraints when interpreting art. The conventional borders that confined artists' imagination have been revolutionised, incubating an immersive realm wherein you command your vantage point. VR has allowed us to unlock an unprecedented level of depth and meaning by stripping away the barriers of physicality. Artistic experiences are no longer tethered to static imagery on canvas but have become dynamic arenas bustling with complex narratives and emotional provocations. This redefining of the realms of possibility constitutes an enormous stride in our collective artistic odyssey.

11.2. Virtual Reality: The Unconventional Muse

Part of VR's most remarkable influence on art has been its metamorphosis into an unconventional muse. Its technological mystique has lured artists into uncharted territories, coaxing them into unveiling new layers of creativity. VR has lent its signature panoramic perspective to art, fostering a renewed artistic dialogue between the creator, the artwork, and the observer.

11.3. Unraveling Art Accessibility and Inclusion

In addition to redefining the boundaries of artists' creations, VR has also democratized the art experience by granting universal access. Art is no longer confined to the elite or closed walls of institutions; everyone with an internet connection can now transcend geographical constraints. Furthermore, it has bolstered inclusion by widening the cultural representation in art and creating spaces for marginalized voices. VR has certainly rewritten the norms of art dissemination and reception, fostering a fairer, more inclusive artistic landscape.

11.4. The Artistic Renaissance: A Beneficiary of Technological Advancements

Virtual reality's prowess has monumentally impacted the art world by culminating in an almost renaissance-like overhaul. The transformation mirrors the democratization of the internet and how it has been a catalyst in opening up the world to information. The ubiquity of VR-ready devices has made high-quality art experiences accessible, ensuring that art gets the amplification and recognition it deserves.

11.5. The Path Ahead: Augmented Reality and Beyond

The potential for technology's expansion within the realm of art is limitless. The emergence of augmented reality (AR), Mixed Reality (MR), and other immersive technologies promise to further disrupt traditional ideas of art and augment our experiences. Consequently, we stand on the cusp of a future where art and technology are inseparable, where creativity bleeds into technology, touching lives, and fostering a more inclusive creative community worldwide.

To conclude, the intersection of art and technology in the age of virtual reality is not just about the perpetuation of a new art medium. It's about redefining how we create, perceive, and interact with art. It's about opening up the world of art to those who have been sidelined. Through the lens of this powerful intersection, the human experience gets a more profound and nuanced reality. So, as the chapters of this novel synergy continue to unfold, we must ensure that we embrace this transformative journey by learning, adapting, and evolving alongside these incredible advancements. The future blooms with promise, and it waits for no one. Let us stride forth and unlock the potential that this exciting junction of art and technology presents.